PARIS 2000+   NEW ARCHITECTURE

NEW ARCHITECTURE   **SAM LUBELL**   PREFACE BY AXEL SOWA

PARIS 2000+

THE MONACELLI PRESS

Acknowledgments

I would like to thank all the architects featured
in this book for their helpfulness, wisdom, and
inspiration, and for sharing their brilliant work.
Moreover, Gianfranco Monacelli, Andrea
Monfried, Elizabeth White, Stacee Lawrence, and
David Blankenship all deserve many thanks for
their phenomenal skill and patience in making
the book a reality. For their insights I am grateful
to Axel Sowa (who also wrote an exceptional
preface), Dominique Alba, Francis Rambert, Bruno
Fortier, Dominique Perrault, Helen Schwoerer,
Jean-Louis Cohen, and Ariela Katz. I am indebted
to the book's photographers—who always
amaze me—for their stunning images. And of
course I'd like to express my gratitude to Carri and
my family for giving me love, inspiration, and
confidence, even from across the ocean.

First published in the United States of America in 2007 by
The Monacelli Press, Inc.
611 Broadway, New York, New York 10012

Copyright © 2007 by The Monacelli Press, Inc.

Library of Congress Cataloging-in-Publication Data

Lubell, Sam.
Paris 2000+ : new architecture / Sam Lubell; preface by Axel Sowa.
p. cm.
Includes index.
ISBN 978-1-58093-190-8 (hardcover)
1. Architecture—France—Paris—21st century.
2. Paris (France)—Buildings, structures, etc. I. Title.
NA1050.L83 2007
720.944'361090511—dc22
2007011113

Printed and bound in China

Designed by David Blankenship

For thirteen centuries, Paris has been the capital of France, but many consider that the city was also the world capital during the nineteenth century. Today, the city still displays the characteristic features of the significant modernization orchestrated by Baron Georges-Eugène Haussmann under Napoleon III. The layout and the embellishment of boulevards, the design of squares and canals, the construction of great public buildings such as the stock exchange, the Opéra, churches, schools, libraries, and covered markets all contributed to an urban idea that combined convention with splendor, the monumental with the utilitarian. Succeeding generations of visionaries, city planners, and architects have had difficulty surpassing this effort. The city remains only the capital of a bygone era. It resists all change. Parisian modernity is manifestly not a matter of construction. In the middle of the twentieth century, Paris had 2.8 million inhabitants, half of whom lived in housing without toilets or baths. Paris makes even the most energetic of builders wait; its inertia frustrates their activism and their visionary ideas.

In hindsight, the great accomplishments of the twentieth century—the markets, la Défense, or the neighborhoods of high-rises like Beaugrenelle, the Olympiades, and Maine-Montparnasse—represent, above all else, dullness and incomprehension. These large-scale modern projects are awkward transplants with no relation to their neighborhoods, withdrawn into themselves, that have never aroused anyone's enthusiasm. Except for the efficient RER railroad network and an expressway and cultural center that both bear the name of Georges Pompidou, the twentieth century has not left a significant mark on the urban framework shaped 150 years ago.

In our time, at the beginning of the twenty-first century, Paris is foundering in a delirium brought on by its own cultural heritage. The brilliant gilding of the Opéra's grand foyer is restored, museum collections are dusted off, sidewalks are paved with granite, period streetlights are installed, old train stations are refurbished. The errors of the modern era have stifled all desire for experimentation. The Haussmannian ideology imposes itself more than ever, and no one stops to consider alternatives.

Clearly, even after a century of heroic battles, the confrontation between modernists and traditionalists has led to nothing definitive. But the French cultivate paradox. They pride themselves on slowly savoring the products of their land, and also on racing across it by TGV at 200 miles per hour. Anyone wishing to understand Parisian modernity should not search among its architects, city planners, or other modernizers.

The city has, however, given birth to some great modern personalities: Baudelaire, Aragon, Debord, Perec. They feed on boredom, banality, oddities, even on the trite. They do not lay new plans for the city but rather use the existing urban background as a sort of projection screen. They scrutinize the quotidian in search of inspiration. The dreary light of alleys, nature in the park of Buttes-Chaumonts, the stereotype of Haussmannian facades, and the approaches to train stations or subways are their preferred materials. According to their artistic philosophy, the most commonplace items and acts take on an evocative and dreamlike quality; banality and boredom give rise to a potential transfiguration of daily life.

Only a few architects have understood the message of these Parisian flâneurs, drifters, strollers, observers, and poets. The last of the Situationists have gone adrift in search of it, and new Parisian residents have already urged the capital toward its currently disdained suburbs. If those who hold high the torch of Parisian modernity are to be believed, the future of Paris is to be found outside its walls. The metropolitan region, greater Paris, the vast suburbs—this is the terra incognita, a psychogeographic area that asks to be discovered. Freeway interchanges, bus stations, large apartment complexes, and commercial centers are called for in plans and projections. The greatest wish for the twenty-first century should be that the highway encircling the city will gradually become a permeable boundary. Let us hope so.

Clockwise from right:
Jakob + MacFarlane, Docks de Paris, Paris Rive Gauche;
Frédéric Borel, École d'Architecture, Paris Val-de-Seine
  (at Paris Rive Gauche);
Christian de Portzamparc, Plan for Masséna quarter,
  Paris Rive Gauche

INTRODUCTION
SAM LUBELL

Paris is a beautiful place, but that legendary beauty makes it one of the most challenging places to build. The dense historic fabric—from grand boulevards to medieval alleys—leaves little room for new architecture and constrains creativity. Architects must battle against conservative officials, change-wary neighbors, stringent urban regulations, and a legendary bureaucracy that frequently slows down or limits projects. Yet despite these obstacles, and despite the perception that the city is an urban museum producing little noteworthy new design, architects continue to flourish there, and the city is emerging as a center of innovation and experiment. In fact, with the best work, the city's challenges inspire unique solutions and better architecture.

The buildings included in this book, all completed since the year 2000, improve on Paris's recent architectural past by employing unortho-dox techniques, materials, and forms that adapt and respond to the city's varied contexts. They combine these attributes with a rich subtlety and a refined sense of texture, composition, and play of light and space. The buildings are not part of an emerging Parisian or French style. Like much contemporary work internationally, their design is driven by intense site-specific research and by individual vision, not by any regional spirit or prevailing dogma.

Most are smaller than François Mitterrand's well-documented *Grands Projets* (also known as *Grands Travaux*), the most visible buildings of Paris's last major wave of construction. Many have been built along the edges of the city and in its immediate suburbs, away from visitors' eyes. Only one, Jean Nouvel's Musée du Quai Branly, is a major new cultural institution. This begins to explain why so few people know about them.

Whatever is being created, it hasn't come without struggle. Opportunities for designing buildings in the historic center are very limited. Competitions, which are mandatory for all public projects, draw hundreds of submissions. "You certainly have to have patience," says Roland Oberhofer, an architect at Paris-based Atelier Seraji. As the economy has privatized and politicians have less appetite for *Grands Projets*, the government, the city's largest client, has fewer commissions to offer.

Outside of infill projects and renovations, the best design opportunities are in the often-unwelcoming peripheral arrondissements (neighborhoods) and closest suburbs. Huge sums are being poured into massive new development zones. These include Paris Rive Gauche, a new development in a former industrial area in the city's southeast; Paris Nord, the Gare du Nord station's former rail yard to the north; and Boulogne-Billancourt, formerly the site of Renault's massive car factories to the southwest.

For the rare commissions awarded in the city center, the weight of history and of urban regulation can limit style and scale. For instance, the Ministry of Culture's Architectes des Bâtiments de France (ABF) must approve projects involving any building located within 150 meters of a historic monument. In Paris this is basically every project. The agency is charged with ensuring that the character, materials, and construction techniques of new architecture fit with the historic neighborhood. The application and approval process is notoriously slow, and when projects pass, contractors often resist non-traditional building methods and materials.

Residents, preservationists, and politicians are conservative about maintaining the look and feel of the neighborhoods. The memories of insensitive demolitions, like the one that destroyed the mythic Les Halles market in the center of the city, are still haunting. Neighborhood groups loudly protested Toyo Ito's recent Cognacq-Jay Hospital in the 15th arrondissement, although it is now one of the least obtrusive modern buildings in the city. Bureaucratic stalling helped convince French millionaire François Pinault to move the contemporary art museum he had planned on the Ile Seguin to the Palazzo Grassi in Venice. Architect Francis Soler remembers that historic preservation groups labeled his contemporary Ministry of Culture offices as "anarchic." Francis Rambert, director of the Cité de l'Architecture et du Patrimoine, Paris's large new architecture center, says the climate is improving, but that it is still "very, very regressive."

Some recent projects have hurt the cause of contemporary architecture. The most visible examples are the *Grands Projets*, which constituted only a small percentage of recent work in the city, but got most of the attention. While I. M. Pei's Pyramide du Louvre has now been accepted, the same cannot be said for Perrault's Bibliothèque Mitterrand (1996), Carlos Ott's Opéra Bastille (1989), and Johann Otto von Spreckelsen's Grand Arche de La Défense (1989). Many French attacked these as ego-driven, ostentatious, context ignoring, and poorly conceived. Beyond the *Grands Projets*, much of the work of the last twenty years stems from rationalist, practical schools of thought and has been limited by strict building codes and a small palette of materials. As a result, the architecture is heavy, blocky, uniform, and repetitive, embellished with grand, but often empty gestures. "People here say, 'If that's modernity, we don't want it,'" Soler comments. Near the periphery and outside the city, the projects are even less attractive and less habitable. Efforts to lighten or enliven facades are abandoned, and massive scales struggle to maintain a sense of comfort or humanity.

While international architects like Frank Gehry and Morphosis have won recent Paris commissions, the struggle of building in the city has become too difficult for many of France's best-known architects, who have begun looking elsewhere for more fertile markets. Paul Andreu, architect of Charles de Gaulle Airport Terminal 2A and several other notable Paris buildings, has not built in the French capital since that airport project was completed in 1999. He is now designing projects in Beijing, Shanghai, Macau, and Chengdu, China. Perrault, who has built at least ten projects in Paris, has not finished a work in the city since the year 2000. He is currently working on four projects in Spain. Odile Decq is completing four projects in Italy, but none in Paris, while Renzo Piano, who has an office in Paris, is currently not working in France, although he did complete the EMI Music France Headquarters, featured in this book, in 2000.

Despite the challenges, architects working in Paris have not only survived but thrived. With many famous French architects working elsewhere, newer, less well-known firms have quickly filled in the gaps. They include Manuelle Gautrand, Chaix & Morel, Périphériques, Jacques Moussafir, Beckmann N'Thépé, Edouard François, and Olivier Brochet. Their best work, as Rambert puts it, is less concerned with grandeur, ego, and theory, and more obsessed with research, urbanity, context, and, of course, architecture. In finding specific, atypical solutions to their environments—be they dense, historic areas that leave little room for manipulation or bleak urban wastelands that offer little contextual inspiration—these architects exceed expectations.

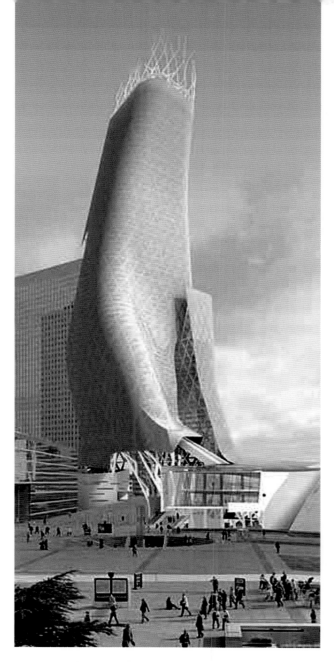

Clockwise from left:
Morphosis, Phare Tower, La Défense;
Atelier Seraji, Student Housing, 15th arrondissement;
Dominique Perrault, Office Building, Boulogne-Billancourt;
Frank Gehry, Louis Vuitton Foundation for Creation,
Bois de Boulogne

This is their style: an interaction with Paris that reflects the city intrinsically, not explicitly. They overcome site limitations by dramatically building forms and plans. Jean Nouvel raised the entire Musée du Quai Branly on large steel columns, making room for an expansive, rolling new garden near the Seine. In order to increase natural light and provide separation between home and work life within a uniform street grid, Christophe Lab raised his living space a full story above his new studio via steel armature. To increase classroom space in a small building, Moussafir cantilevered new classrooms over the edge of his Paris 8 arts school in Saint Denis. Lacaton & Vassal exploited a very restricted budget for the renovation of the Palais de Tokyo by leaving the building practically as is, in order to take advantage of its "splendid" state of deterioration. Forced to limit interior surface area in the new Citroën showroom on the Champs-Elysées, Manuelle Gautrand created a massive void in the front of the building that unifies the space and emphasizes its dramatic height.

"We should never be afraid to test the authorities," says architect Edouard François, who recently completed the edgy Hôtel Fouquet's Barrière near the Champs-Elysées.

Another strategy is the exploration of new materials and construction techniques. LIN created a new type of fiberglass concrete to provide an ultra-thin and malleable surface that wraps around the interior of the Pavillon de l'Arsenal. Shigeru Ban utilized only PVC, plywood, and cardboard to create a dramatic but unobtrusive temporary office at the Centre Pompidou. Jakob + MacFarlane developed structural honeycomb panels faced in resin-coated aluminum to produce lightweight angled fins to line the exhibition hall of its Renault press headquarters. The fins hang in midair, never touching the ground, dramatically shaping the cavernous space. In Périphérique's classroom addition to Pierre et Marie Curie's Jussieu campus in the 5th arrondissement, concrete becomes a light, decorative material, a sharp contrast to the existing 1960s buildings. In the same vein, Nouvel incorporated natural vegetation in the facade of the Musée du Quai Branly.

The completion of these projects is a result of more than just the architects' creativity and tenacity. Many new buildings have been privately financed, a change of patronage in the socialist state of France. Corporate executives have discovered the role architecture can play in increasing profits and enhancing brand image. Meanwhile city and state officials, spurred by broader public awareness and acceptance of contemporary architecture, are promoting innovative design. A symbol of this movement is Soler's new headquarters for the Ministry of Culture, which unites the architecture of three time periods under a fascinating metal skin and replaces the ministry's closed, outdated offices in the Palais Royale with transparent, modern amenities. The city government has begun to relax strict zoning and building regulations. Mayor Bertrand Delanoë's recently released PLU (Plan Local d'Urbanisme) relates planning to specific localities rather than applying the same principles to the entire city. The mayor, who is still criticized by many architects for talking a lot but playing it safe, has nonetheless revamped the architectural competitions process within several city agencies. He promoted an ideas competition for the Les Halles marketplace in the city center (although the winning design, a fairly conservative plan by David Mangin, was attacked by most architects, and the area's future is still unclear), and he recently supported the competition that resulted in Morphosis's Phare tower, a curved, shifting building with a double glass skin and a crowning wind farm.

Yet despite the success of the city's recent and upcoming architecture, many questions remain. One involves the global nature of French architecture. Since the newest Parisian buildings have little cohesion to history or region, how can they achieve a sense of place? A great-looking building in Paris looks a lot like a great-looking building in Amsterdam or New York. "This is the state of architecture everywhere," says Bruno Fortier, a noted French architect and urbanist. "There is no longer a Swiss style, or Chinese style, or German style." Moussafir, one of the rising stars in the country, insists that one can respect the spirit of a place, and enhance its peculiarities without having to employ the same architecture and the same materials as everyone else in the city. Daniel Claris, an architect at Paris-based AREP, adds that architecture needs to reflect its time: "Each generation needs to find its liberty of expression." The city, he adds, needs to evolve: "In the end, the biggest thing is to respect the city."

Indeed, some of the most creative new projects are able to help maintain either the strict visual unity or the intimate human character that makes the city so special. But many critics feel this type of absorption helps keep Paris a museum that is trapped in time, not a dynamic capital. Many French architects hope that Paris will take measures like lightening restrictions in historic zones and lifting its ban on skyscrapers within the city limits. "Paris can't be against everything that is new. It needs to live and modernize and improve and enlarge. Otherwise we will see decadence and degradation," says Christian de Portzamparc. He has had a chance to make some changes. As the master planner for much of Seine Rive Gauche and other new development zones, he has fought hard for open plan urbanism, which breaks holes into the strict Parisian street grid, opening it, he says, to light and air and design freedom.

Similar criticisms have been leveled at other major historically rich cities like Rome, Florence, Prague, and Vienna, where the tension between maintaining legendary cityscapes and moving forward always makes for compelling headlines. Richard Meier spent years battling conservative Italian deputy cultural minister Vittorio Sgarbi over his Ara Pacis pavilion (2006), located in city's historic center. Enrique Miralles's Scottish Parliament (2004) in Edinburgh has won critical acclaim, but the Scottish public have attacked the building incessantly. Modern plans for several town centers in France have been scuttled in favor of traditional ones.

Perhaps bigger questions lie outside Paris, where it is still unclear whether architecture can save what Fortier calls the ugliest periphery in Europe (this area also presents the biggest redevelopment opportunity in France). Exceptions like Ibos & Vitart's striking fire station in the rough suburb of Nanterre cannot transform entire neighborhoods, although they can sometimes lead to better buildings around them. Still, there must be a concerted effort. One problem, Fortier points out, is that because many buildings here are cooperatively owned, massive transformation becomes much more difficult. A larger challenge is that the zones have few resources. In area, Paris is one of the smaller world capitals, and the city limits have remained unchanged since the nineteenth century. This concentrates resources within those boundaries and leaves little tax base or government oversight for its struggling neighbors.

The dynamism of recent Paris buildings and the ability of designers to take advantage of the city's challenges will not solve these issues. But it can be a starting point, a model for ways that intensive research and creative solutions can tackle complex urban problems. The struggle gives the buildings themselves true originality and intimately ties them to the city. The buildings reflect the city's struggle to balance the forces of its past and its present; its core and its periphery. They reflect its struggle to decipher its culture in a globalized, multicultural world. The solution to these issues is not to run from them. It is to take advantage of them.

David Mangin, Les Halles, site plan and interior rendering

JEAN NOUVEL
MUSÉE
DU QUAI BRANLY
2006

Jean Nouvel's Musée du Quai Branly, displaying indigenous art from Africa, Oceania, Asia, and the Americas, is the most conspicuous, ambitious new building created in Paris since the Centre Pompidou.

Raised 32 feet on steel pilotis above a dense, winding garden, and slightly angled in elevation to follow the curves of the Seine and the rue de l'Université, the 420,000-square-foot building includes exhibition space, a library, offices, theaters, viewable reserve space, and a café. The predominantly red and black steel-clad building is meant to evoke a bridge suspended in a forest.

Inside, Nouvel designed the space to eschew the rigid typology of most Western art museums. An open, 80-foot-tall space, including overhanging galleries, contains the collections. To enter, visitors ascend a glazed spiral walkway, clad on its exterior with white steel brise-soleils. The exhibition space is clad to its south with a grid of square, steel-framed windows, covered with a dotted film that produces a rhythmical play of light. To the north, a curtain wall is composed of diamond-shaped windows covered with a photographic film depicting lush landscapes. Boxes of various sizes and colors project from the north facade, cantilevering over the garden.

The interior is theatrical. The exhibition area is divided by region, but its low walls allow visitors a broader (and sometimes overwhelming) view. Pinpoints of light shine into large glass vitrines. Objects often hang by thin filaments, appearing to float inside. Eerie reflections of

nearby items appear on the glazing, while shiny resin floors catch the gleam of overhead lights. The collections—including masks, statues, jewels, musical instruments, native costumes, head-dresses, and earthenware—are exciting, but the descriptive text that accompanies the objects is often meager or left in shadow.

One of the goals, says project architect Didier Brault, was to create an organic aesthetic suggestive of the rural environments where most of the objects were created. The pastoral images on north-facing windows depict regions represented in the museum. Floor and ceiling heights gradually move up and down like hills and valleys, and a leather-lined walkway, known as the snake, threads its way like a river through the galleries. Such risky flourishes are captivating but sometimes border on the overdramatic. The far north-facing galleries, fit into the boxes protruding from the north facade, are a notable success. The often-unexpected spaces vary between cavernous displays and tiny cubbyholes, each tailored to the art inside.

The still-expanding gardens cover most of the ground level, insulated from riverside traffic by a wall of glass. The "vegetal wall" of the museum offices, with over fifteen thousand plants slipped into pockets of thick felt, sits just west. To the south of the exhibition building, an elegant narrow rectilinear glass building contains a gift shop, studios, and more offices.

The museum's reddish colors, explains Brault, were chosen based on intuition. This seems indicative of an overall aesthetic that appears somewhat disparate and unrooted. Nonetheless, the floating building quickly captures the imagination, and this dynamic museum structure is like no other in Paris or the world.

23

CHRISTIAN
DE PORTZAMPARC
LE MONDE
HEADQUARTERS
2005

In planning its new headquarters in the south of the city, the French newspaper Le Monde wanted not only to enlarge and modernize its facilities, but also, as architect Christian de Portzamparc says, to create "a landmark in the city." His solution was not subtle: a double-layer glass facade to which a giant replica of the front page of the paper is affixed via a semitransparent adhesive. The mock-up's typography imitates the real paper, and it even contains a cartoon designed by the caricaturist Jean Plantureux, known as Plantu. The text is an essay by Victor Hugo about the importance of the free press. The giant broadsheet works not only as an advertisement—it can be seen clearly from the street and the passing elevated Métro—but also as a solar shade for the south-facing surface.

The 195,000-square-foot project is a clever and clear transformation of what was a nondescript 1970s office building that Air France once owned. De Portzamparc widened the footprint by about twenty feet to meet the street grid, exceeding zoning regulations. To compensate, he reduced the height, setting the topmost floors behind the facade at a roughly 45 degree angle. He clad the structure with an interesting, if not beautiful, folded aluminum skin composed of alternately colored and textured panels and irregularly spaced windows.

Inside, De Portzamparc gutted most of the existing building. He moved the elevator banks toward the perimeter to make room for a three-story glass-roofed entrance atrium. Plexiglas columns filled with air bubbles, recalling vertical tanks of water, energize the space. At the north end of the atrium, horizontal white, ivory, and brown aluminum panels form an arresting screen in front a series of glass bridges that connect offices. Under this composition, a long, curved mirror creates the illusion of being able to see the sky from the lobby.

On the top two levels Elizabeth de Portzamparc, who heads her own design firm, designed a dynamic cafeteria, restaurant, and winter garden. Warm, recessed lighting, bright colors, sensuous curves, polished woods, and projecting forms covered in metal mesh make this area one of the building's important features. The newspaper's office spaces are fairly conventional, but they contain new computer systems, about 13,000 square feet of additional space, and a large theater, an exercise room, and an interior garden to the east of the atrium. A roof deck with a brise-soleil of curved green, yellow, and white aluminum posts accommodates meetings and less formal gatherings.

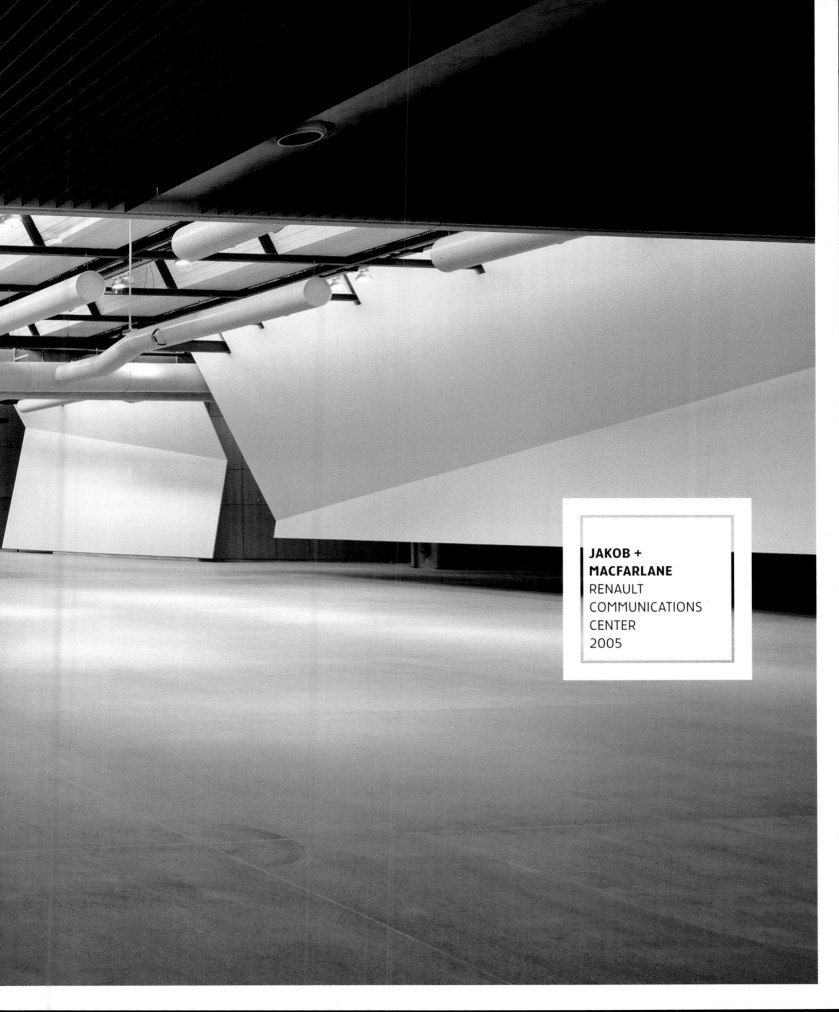

JAKOB +
MACFARLANE
RENAULT
COMMUNICATIONS
CENTER
2005

Paris-based Jakob + MacFarlane, designers of Georges Restaurant at the Centre Pompidou, took on a far bigger task as winners of a 2000 competition to remake the Renault car factory in Boulogne-Billancourt into the company's corporate communications center. Claude Vasconi designed the original 160,000-square-foot brick, glass, and steel building in the early 1980s.

The firm decided to maintain the exterior, which steps up from 100 to 200 to 300 feet from west to east and incorporates large skylights, which have been fitted with new windows. A glass atrium between the factory's two buildings creates a new lobby. The open plan allowed the architects to create completely new facilities inside. Interventions have gray or white surfaces and remain physically unconnected to the original building. The new complex is divided into three parts: a 40,000-square-foot exhibition hall, executive offices, conference rooms, and a car garage to the north; creative offices and theaters to the south; and the lobby and offices to the west.

The firm retained the factory's open environment, exposing mechanical systems and installing metal catwalks. White, slightly folded walls echo the slanted windows that appear along much of the original facade. The new walls are made of unique structural honeycomb panels faced in resin-coated aluminum and have been set off by wood paneling in some areas. They appear quite light, especially in the large exhibition area, where they hang down from the ceiling, not touching the ground, dramatically shaping the cavernous space. As Brendan MacFarlane explains, the blank white surfaces of this space defer to the main attraction: the cars. Folding glass walls on either side allow the space to join or be sealed off from the rest of the building, while a giant new glass curtain to the east lets natural light flow in. This structure can be dismantled to accommodate the entry of large trucks or exhibitions.

Other interesting structural elements support the display of cars inside the building. Four different-sized theaters are fitted with round, revolving stages, and folding ramps or sliding walls allow the cars inside. A massive elevator in the northeast section of the building brings cars down from the parking garage above. Cars are driven through the space for exhibition placement, a strange sight inside a corporate office.

The neighborhood, which once housed Renault's entire factory complex, is about to see an explosion of new construction. Foster + Partners is building an office building just next door, and the Ile Seguin, across the river, is becoming a major cultural, business, and science center. Eventually, a bridge will link the island to the factory site.

ARTE CHARPENTIER
& ASSOCIÉS
STATION MÉTÉOR
GARE ST. LAZARE
2003

It's not often that Paris builds a Métro line. In fact the "Météor," connecting the St. Lazare station with the Bibliothèque Mitterrand, was the first new route constructed in more than fifty years. Seizing the opportunity, Paris-based Arte Charpentier convinced officials to deviate from their customary architect/engineer hierarchy, allowing them to design, rather than just "decorate" one of the line's two terminus stations, under the Gare St. Lazare. The solution introduces large, open areas, replacing the maze of tunnels that often characterize the Métro. The legibility of the space, along with clear signage, directs people to several lines and exits in what is, says firm associate Pierre Clement, "basically a city underground."

The new street-level entrance is dramatic: a low, elliptical glass structure set within Gare St. Lazare's Cour du Rome. Parisians now refer to it as the *lentille*, or lentil. The dynamic shape, formed with a bidirectional steel frame, catches reflections during the day and glows at night. Its curvaceous form, Clement points out, interacts with the intricate embellishments of the neighborhood better than any staid modernist cube. Through this opening—loosely inspired by Hector Guimard's art nouveau Métro entrances—daylight penetrates three levels into the five-floor station, further facilitated by translucent glass

stairs. Interior spaces are clad with warm-colored local stone, polished concrete, and railings and fixtures of stainless steel. The minimalist but welcoming aesthetic accentuates the large volumes and minimizes confusion. An atrium space under the *lentille* centralizes circulation; it is highlighted by a massive circular staircase and by a giant clock built into its stone floor.

At track level, exposed concrete ceilings arch over the tracks; walls are covered with frosted glass, a modern interpretation of the tile embellishments in the older stations. Sound insulation on the ceilings and on the tracks themselves make the area quite comfortable for the rush of commuters. The project took five years to complete, and the work did not interrupt service to the station's multiple lines.

MANUELLE GAUTRAND
CITROËN
SHOWROOM
2006

When André Citroën first built his car showroom on the Champs-Elysées in the 1920s, the minimalist, rectilinear building, with its giant glass facade, was one of the most advanced structures of its time. In updating it, the image-conscious company wanted to create something equally advanced. Gautrand's new showroom, a commission won in competition in 2001, does not disappoint. It is easily the most daring structure in this area of Paris.

Like the original space, the new building's sculpted facade begins as a glass square in a steel frame. But moving upward, the tall facade takes the form of Renault's famous triangular symbol, the chevron. The glass symbol is lined with bright red film that is more visible inside, since executives were worried about the facade being too splashy. Farther up, the shape begins to deform into diamond shapes that project audaciously from the plane of the facade. It then bends above the building and curves back down the other side. The facade's curves, and its glass and steel fabrication, are meant to echo the design of the company's cars. Along the court-yard, the windows are alternately clear and frosted, allowing glimpses of the surroundings but minimizing interior heat.

Inside, Gautrand has designed what is essentially a large open staircase curving around a central vertical progression of circular steel platforms. The rotating platforms are suspended either from the structure's concrete slabs or from a red steel mast near the back of the space. Display floors are covered with sleek white resin, and sliding glass railings in front of the cars maximize views but protect the merchandise. On the underside of the platforms, three-dimensional arrays of mirrored triangles, an allusion to the tectonic facade, reflect the cars underneath.

Gautrand added several feet to the original height, but strict space regulations required maintaining the same overall square footage. Hence, she created a massive void fronting the stairway and platforms. The void, a function of necessity, gives the space unity and grandeur and allows red light to penetrate from the facade all the way to the stairs on the other side of the space. It also allows cars to be hoisted up to the display platforms on a lift housed in the basement. Citroën's red and white palette is the only color in the minimal interior, whether on tinted red windows, bright red car platforms, or glossy white walls. This structure is tiny compared with massive new showrooms for BMW and Mercedes, but it is an important symbol of French companies' new embrace of architecture to improve image—or in this case, to become the image itself.

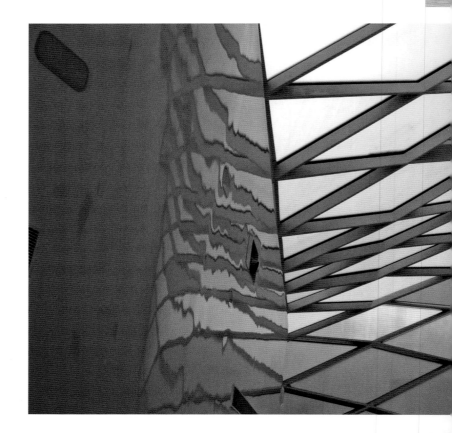

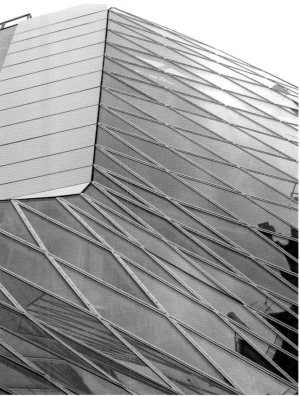

LIN
PAVILLON
DE L'ARSENAL
2003

In 2003 LIN, a firm based in Paris and Berlin, finished a project important to all lovers of contemporary Paris architecture: the permanent exhibition space of the Pavillon de l'Arsenal, a center dedicated to architecture and urban planning in Paris. Originally a factory workshop for the Samaritaine department store, the building was converted into an exhibition center by French architects Reichen & Robert in 1987. For this iteration, the Pavillon's directors wanted a much more contemporary design that would unify an area that had been cluttered with walls, partitions, and bridges and separated into different rooms.

The firm clad the 7,100-square-foot exhibition space with an 18-millimeter-thick silver-colored fiber-reinforced concrete skin that curves up from the floors to form its own walls, enveloping the space. LIN partner Finn Geipel points out that the firm developed the self-supporting material specifically for the project.

The dark surface and the exposed concrete and cast-iron columns create both an industrial and futuristic aesthetic and provide a neutral, fluid backdrop for the installation. Walls were removed to create a single space, but the firm retained the triple-height entrance, which emphasized the massive barrel-vaulted ceiling pierced with a grand skylight.

The permanent exhibition, "Paris: A Guided Tour; The City, Past and Present," includes models, charts, maps, and pictures, and the firm developed a self-lighting electrolucent membrane to make some of the maps and pictures glow. Slides and films of projects are projected onto the new concrete skin. On the floor above are architect-built temporary exhibitions, collections of images and models of future city projects, and a curving red-glass and neon video library recently designed by Paris architect Christian Biecher.

CHAIX & MOREL
PETIT PALAIS
2005

The Petit Palais, constructed as the Palace of Fine Arts for the Exposition Universelle in 1900, is a grand building in an eclectic style. When first completed, architect Charles Giraud's facade was embellished with neoclassical balustrades and columns, a massive gilded doorway, and rows of stone vases along the roofline. Large skylights—then a new technology—and large bay windows brought daylight inside. Over the years, false ceilings, blinkered windows, and partitions ruined the effect, and the museum had fallen into disrepair by the turn of the millennium. Paris firm Chaix & Morel's extensive renovation restored the building to its original light-filled state and almost doubled the exhibition and office space, with new galleries built in a contemporary style.

The firm orchestrated the cleaning and restoration of the facade, mosaic tile floors, and giant ceiling murals; installed a new ventilation system; and replaced much of the deteriorated stonework, including replacing all the vases with molded copies. But perhaps most important was the focus on restoring light to the interior. The architects removed several false ceilings and installed a system that draws light through a series of transparent and semitransparent skylights along the length of the north wing. Natural light is supplemented with fluorescent lighting that is activated when exterior light levels drop. But looking up from the floor, one sees only a minimalist grid of translucent glass, which provides a warm glow. Light also enters through large garden-facing windows, which had become solid niches during previous renovations. Similar niches have been opened up throughout the building. Circular artificial light wells in the first floor bring light to what was once a dark exhibition and storage space; fluorescent light shines up from the wells into the main lobby.

Although the museum—accessible via a grand west-facing stairway leading to its second floor—already had some underground galleries, two additional floors were excavated under the garden. The two basements contain technical and conservation facilities, opening up room on the ground floor of the existing museum—which had become a characterless zone used for storage and conservation—as modern new gallery space. Hundreds of items once in storage are now on display, increasing the total number of works shown from 850 pieces to 1,300. In total, the museum now has 75,000 square feet of new exhibition space. The re-formed single-level spaces on the first floor are clad with cherry wood, granite, patinated metal, and plaster. The interiors are warm and contemporary, although not necessarily, as the firm puts it, "noble," a popular description in France to describe that which is weighty and, often, expensive. Nonetheless, the new zones provide a good counterpoint to the cavernous classical areas in the rest of the museum, which have been renovated, relit, and in many cases set with freestanding glass vitrines. The firm also created a modern new auditorium, restaurant, and gift shop, as well as airy new offices above the south wing, more than doubling the museum's office space.

FRANCIS SOLER
MINISTRY OF CULTURE
2005

Perhaps the most pressing question in French architecture today is how old and new can exist side by side. Paris architect Francis Soler took this challenge one step further by proposing to combine them in the same structure. His new Ministry of Culture building on Rue St.-Honoré in the 1st arrondissement, just blocks from the Louvre, unites a Renaissance-style 1920s department store and an attached modernist 1950s structure to its north (renovated in the 1980s) within the skeleton of a laser-cut stainless steel screen composed of more than 4,000 thin panels. The screen acts as a unifying element, a hypnotic facade, and a solar shade. The light-weight structure slopes inward at the top, and its curving outline, which Soler likens to static on a television set, is an abstraction of a Renaissance painting and intended as a symbol in itself of the merger of old and new. "I wanted to create a new kind of architecture out of the country's patrimony," says Soler. "It's not a juxtaposition— it's a superposition."

Behind the screen, the firm gutted much of the interior, inserting a collection of loftlike but unremarkable offices composed of floor-to-ceiling steel partitions fitted with double glazing. The 1920s stone facade remains intact, whereas the 1950s building was fitted with a grid of vertical windows with silver-colored aluminum frames. This nine-story structure is connected to the seven-story 1920s building via hallways that step down to accommodate the differences in floor level. Painted patterns in the lobby imitate the exterior screen, and the ceiling is fitted with thin hanging metal filaments.

The firm demolished a building along rue de Bons Enfants on the west side of the project to create a leafy, contemporary-style U-shaped courtyard. The court allows natural light into offices and furnishes impressive views of Paris's historic center.

The new Ministry building unites various cultural departments that had been scattered around the quarter. The headquarters had been housed in the beautiful but outdated and very closed-off offices of the Palais Royale.

PÉRIPHÉRIQUES
JUSSIEU CAMPUS
EXTENSION
2006

The building's partitioned glass curtain facade is covered with an intricate anodized aluminum screen perforated with lively patterns of different-sized circles. The thin frontage animates the facade, creates shimmering light effects inside, and provides natural ventilation and solar shading for the non-air-conditioned structure. Near the northwest corner of the building the screen disappears, and colorful glass-enclosed balconies mimic the forms of surrounding buildings.

Whereas most campus buildings have low, enclosed entrance areas, this structure is essentially a giant atrium, with every floor visible from the bright orange lobby. Light pours in through a glass ceiling. Concrete walls, colored in neon yellow, pink, orange, and blue, are cut with ovular perforations. Behind them are walkways and brightly colored classrooms arranged around the perimeter of the building. The thin concrete surfaces are not load-bearing—concrete columns closer have that function—and they never touch the ground, floating just above the floor. Colors identify each department, another way-finding strategy. The open space is crisscrossed by a fascinating barrage of steel-framed concrete bridges and escalators that link various levels both vertically and horizontally, creating one of the most animated interior spaces in the city.

Walking through Pierre et Marie Curie University on the east end of the Latin Quarter, you see quickly that many buildings are clad with thick concrete walls and slabs, employed in a depressing 1960s housing block kind of way. For the aging campus's new classroom building, Périphériques again used concrete, but this time as a light, sculptural, even playful element.

The six-story, 180,000-square-foot project, located on the east side of the superblock campus, respects architect Edouard Albert's 1960s grid plan as well as the massing and scale of the surrounding buildings. But unlike these structures, which have only nondescript service entrances below the campus's elevated concrete plaza, the new building has a bright orange entry court that folds up like origami from ground level to its front doors. The area not only invites students to the building but also becomes a clear route to other parts of campus.

MICHELE SAEE
PUBLICIS DRUGSTORE
2004

In 2000 Los Angeles–based architect Michele Saee won a competition to renovate the legendary Publicis drugstore at the west end of the Champs-Elysées. The store's beautiful Haussmann-era building burned down in the early 1970s and was replaced in 1972 with a concrete and mirrored structure that added little to the bustling streetscape.

For budgetary and practical reasons, Saee could not tear down the 1970s facade. Instead he created a "transparent and ephemeral" new surface—evocative of the vast waves of pedestrian and automobile movement on the Champs-Elysées—that could coexist with the old. "Their intentions got melted into one," says Saee of the two facades. The arrangement lends lightness and movement to the heavy building and injects excitement into this section of the Champs Elysées, where contemporary new stores seem to pop up every month.

The architect wrapped the facade in curved, overlapping glass panels. The clear, low-iron screens, glued to twisting aluminum fins, are held in a series of curving steel armatures, which are bolted to the concrete frame. A vertical, spiraling corner element, which appears to float in midair, cantilevers off the columns of the north-facing facade like a giant sculpture. The curvaceous facade, captured especially well through dynamic lighting at night, evokes flux and resembles a roller coaster making its way up and down the building's surface.

Inside, Saee renovated five floors, including an employee café, bathrooms, and offices. The most-visited areas are the retail spaces on the first floor and basement, which contain a restaurant, newsstand, wine store, book store, gift store, clothing store, and more. Ironically, the pharmacy itself occupies a small white room that seems somewhat like an afterthought.

The plan of the brightly colored spaces mimics the overlapping facade panels, with floors, walls, counters, stair railings, and even the ring mesh-covered ceilings curving left, right, upward, and downward. Curving basement ceilings, made with plaster molds, are lit with tiny LED stars. Wavy transparent or translucent glass dividers—some extending from the ceiling, others from the floor—partition the open space.

AREP
GARE DU NORD, ÎLE DE
FRANCE INTERCHANGE
& MAGENTA STATION
(RER)
2002

AREP—a public/private company developed by French transportation officials—felt it appropriate to employ old forms with new materials when replacing a treasured turn-of-the-century landmark that had been a victim of 1960s urban renewal. The landmark in question was a beautiful glass, iron, and wood commuter station just east of the Gare du Nord (below). The building had been almost completely torn down and replaced with a brutalist-style parking garage and underground shopping interchange (bottom).

AREP decided to reverse history, tearing down the 1960s structure and reshaping it to resemble the old station. The firm rebuilt the original pitched roof with large, steel-framed glass panels. Most of the tall, thin support columns are made of steel and high-strength concrete, although the west side of the new building contains some original iron columns and wood beams. The open space is protected from excess heat with panes of patterned glass on its ceiling; it affords unimpeded views onto the surrounding cityscape, provides natural light during the day, and glows at night. The animated scene behind it and the activity in the small new pedestrian square in front of the building has helped revive the once-deserted street.

Inside, light also penetrates into two new sunken retail and circulation levels. Wood-covered footbridges add warmth and relate to the new AREP-designed RER (line E) station below. The open plan adds coherence to a zone that connects the Métro, two RER lines, and national and international trains.

Wood floors and wood-clad walls at the entry to the new RER line mark the change in function of the space and add a measure of welcome to an environment that burrows almost one hundred feet below street level. Contemporary lighting over the escalators provided by sleek, suspended chandeliers is divided into white for ascending, and red for descending. Copper clads all support infrastructure, while sharply vaulted, dramatically lit exposed-concrete hallways provide circulation to the tracks. A large intermediate hall has windows overlooking the street, allowing daylight in, and the central circulation hall near the entrance to the RER tracks is fitted with large skylights to allow further light penetration. At train level, sound barriers on vaulted concrete ceilings and near rails minimize noise.

PHILIPPE STARCK
KONG RESTAURANT
2003

Located on the top two floors of Paris's chic Kenzo building in the 1st arrondissement, this sleek, übertrendy restaurant, just east of the Seine, has one of the best views of any spot in Paris. The main dining space, on the restaurant's second floor, is surrounded almost completely with floor-to-ceiling curved glass, and visitors get the sensation of floating in a pod above the river, the Pont Neuf, and the oldest part of the city.

The very stylized design offers typical Starck touches such as lime green fluorescent stairways, glossy plastic seats, and purple neon lights behind a sinuous bar. Tension is created by juxtaposing opposites: historical and modern; Eastern and Western; feminine and masculine; elegant and kitsch; natural and urban. Louis XIV–style armchairs sit in front of ancient Asian iconography; seat backs are printed with the heads of both spiky-haired and traditional Asian and European women. Among the humorous touches are Japanese anime cartoons painted by Starck's daughter on the wall of the dining space.

The first floor is designed for mixing and flirting. While the décor is very contemporary, its textures give it a more eclectic look than many of the ultrasleek restaurants in Kong's category. The space centers on a long, rectangular, resin-topped bar glowing with orange light from below and embedded with red orchids. Walls and ceilings are painted in an unfinished style that suggests an artist's studio; floor surfaces recall tiny stones in a Japanese garden; and tables are painted with close-up images of skin. The room is also fitted with a disc-jockey table and a neon violet replica of an eighteenth-century armoire.

By contrast, the second floor dining space is much simpler. It is furnished with small tables, clear plastic seats, and light gray couches, and the only nighttime lighting comes from small tabletop lamps. The interior decoration defers to the view—although there is still a giant geisha mural on the ceiling.

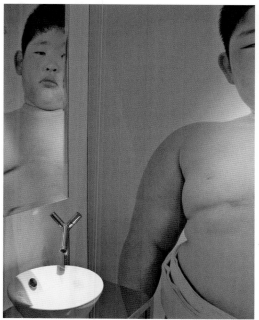

Inventive architects Christophe Lab and Cécile Courtey decided to build a new home and office for themselves in the north of Paris, in the 19th arrondissement. The challenge: they wanted to maintain sufficient separation between home life and work life. The solution: to suspend the striking upper-level living space, by means of a steel armature, above the first- and second-floor studio.

The double-height work studio, whose second-floor spaces overlook the first via metal balconies, receives light through semitranslucent polycarbonate windows and a massive clear skylight that looks up at the studio above. Almost inexplicably, a grand piano sits in the middle of the first floor, between tall steel columns.

The unusual two-story living space, reached via elevator or stairs, is suffused with light, transparency, reflections, and, what the architects like to call "the sense of disorder of our times." A visitor walks through narrow hallways, passing by red, yellow, black, and white walls with triangle, square, and oval-shaped windows. A glass-enclosed patio, with a 2-centimeter-thick glass floor, allows unimpeded views of the neighborhood, but it can feel like a greenhouse in the summer. The kitchen opens to this space through a hydraulically-pivoting horizontal panel.

The 4,600-square-foot building contrasts strikingly with the heavy masonry structures that dominate the neighborhood. The architects call their style "liberté totale," meaning they wish to be influenced by no person or context, just by their imagination. Their only rule is that each building they design must tell a story. The architects describe a house they designed, in Nanterre, to the west of the city, as a suitcase that has been opened on the street. The home and office they designed for themselves, they say, is a house that decided to move (upstairs, away from the office, that is).

RENZO PIANO
BUILDING WORKSHOP
EMI MUSIC FRANCE
HEADQUARTERS
2005

Recording giant EMI's new French headquarters, a cluster of shedlike, steel-framed buildings clad with red terra cotta and topped with a saw-toothed roofline, takes its aesthetic and programmatic cues from the mechanics' workshops that once dominated this neighborhood in the far north of the city.

The three-story, 89,000-square-foot project is organized around a rectangular courtyard, which is lined with trees, benches, tables, and stone pathways. Built on a former bus parking lot, the complex includes four new and two restored buildings containing offices, recording studios, and a small performance space. The ambience is remarkably intimate and peaceful, a characteristic of many Piano projects but seemingly at odds with the record label's brash image. Nevertheless, young, hip employees enjoy what firm architect Alain Gallissian calls a small-scale "village" for music. Offices are divided into clearly separated (but still attached) pavilions, each with its own entrance onto the courtyard. To the west, offices are entered from the street. To the east, they can be reached by a series of small footbridges.

Inside, walkways lined with floor-to-ceiling windows create a central circulation path around the courtyard. Farther from the green space, loft-like offices evoke artisans' and engineers' workshops rather than corporate workplaces. All structure is exposed, including the steel frame and the mechanical ducts, and the aesthetic extends even to the aluminum office furniture.

Large skylights angled at 60 degrees and glass office walls allow light to pour in and give the space an open feel. Four triple-height skylit "patios," scattered throughout the building, serve as conference rooms and meeting places. On the east side of the campus, light wells allow sunshine into basement offices.

On the south side, a renovated workshop building contains a cafeteria, a VIP room, and an intimate performance space for musicians to try out new material. Mechanical systems are tucked into the back of this space, keeping the rest of the complex free of clutter.

ADAM YEDID
PALAIS DE JUSTICE
EXTENSION
2004

In designing a new criminal court inside the Palais de Justice, the country's highest court, Paris architect Adam Yedid chose separation—both stylistic and physical—as the best way to fit in.

The new 6,450-square-foot court, inserted into a narrow courtyard, includes a main trial room, press quarters, judge's chambers, and supplementary offices. The two-story rectangular box is clad with a minimalist facade composed of matte silver aluminum panels that never touch the walls of the original nineteenth-century structure. The composition successfully carries out Yedid's stated goals of injecting modernity into the complex while deferring to and preserving the historic fabric, although its extreme simplicity and necessarily window-free facade (events inside the room cannot be seen by outsiders) recall somewhat the temporary facilities used elsewhere in the complex.

Inside, Yedid continued this discreet, rectilinear vocabulary and utilized cool materials to convey a serious tone. Rust-colored steel forms the bases of tables and podiums; expanded metal covers balconies and an elegant spiral staircase leading to the press balcony; and aluminum panels cover stairways and most walls. Yedid also wanted the space to be "quiet, serene, and even comforting," and he warmed the room with light-colored wood, which clads some panel walls, benches, tabletops, stairs, and floors. Softly lit judge's chambers and offices are decorated in a similar theme.

Natural light enters through narrow angled skylights in the center and back of the court-room. Mechanical systems are located under the building, so the roof maintains a smooth appearance, with the exception of a tall, narrow chimney that reaches to the top of the courtyard.

JACQUES MOUSSAFIR
PARIS 8,
SCHOOL OF ART
2001

Paris architect Jacques Moussafir's new Paris 8 art school transformed a hastily constructed 1981 concrete building, whose cheap terra cotta cladding made it look more like a parking garage than a place of learning. It is located in Saint Denis, a rough suburb of Paris.

The two-floor facility, built into the open plan of the older building, brightens up this bleak environment with unusual solutions. Incorporating spaces for music, dance, photography, and visual arts, its plan is composed of rectangular classrooms and studios arranged at varying angles along a straight, clearly organized circulation corridor. Also askew are the trapezoidal antechambers to the classrooms. These small, brightly colored zones create a clear transition between hall and classroom, add depth and spots of color to the interior, and provide space for students to leave their shoes and bags. Trapezoidal windowsills project from the facade, adding a feeling of depth to the classrooms and framing views of the bleak landscape outside in a unique, photographic way that lends coherence and drama. Very bright green, orange, red, and blue walls identify departments and add life to interiors, an effect heightened when the colors reflect off polished resin floors.

The facade is composed of Cor-Ten steel panels, and their rough, rusted surface reflects the gritty neighborhood. "We didn't want the building to stand out like a lie," Moussafir says. And it does not. The panels project in various directions, a function of the angled window extensions, which gives the facade a much-needed texture and intricacy. A few classrooms also cantilever from the thick concrete frame, providing additional space. These boxlike protrusions, perhaps the building's most interesting feature, were necessary to introduce generous hallways and still meet the program requirements for classroom space.

Herzog & de Meuron's intricate and subtle rue des Suisses public housing apartments, located in the far south of Paris, are a welcome break from the huge, sanitized white and beige blocks that are all too common in the neighborhood and in much of outer Paris. The complex includes three narrow buildings: two along the intersecting rue des Suisses and rue de Jonquoy and one along a courtyard that extends almost 400 feet behind the street. The facility contains fifty-seven apartments in all.

The buildings facing the street are shrouded in dark expanded metal shutters that open accordion-style. The somber uniformity of the composition allows this recent addition to the nineteenth-century street wall to remain almost invisible, drawing attention to itself only by its light gray concrete floor slabs and opened shutters. The buildings bend slightly inward near the entrances, creating subtle visual variety and forming a clear funnel toward the interior courtyard.

The long, narrow garden courtyard is, by contrast, a light, peaceful setting filled with trees, plants, nooks, and pathways. The intimate space, dappled with soft light, feels far from Paris. Along the length of the courtyard is a three-story building faced with curving timber shutters that slide up and down on bowed metal guide rails at the ends of narrow balconies. The firm limited this building to three stories to keep families close to the garden and to maintain an intimate scale and access to natural light. A planted roof adds to the distance from urban chaos and eases water runoff.

The complex's narrow apartments receive natural light from two sides through a continuous row of vertical rectangular windows, and first-floor courtyard apartments have the added benefit of private backyards. Vines growing in a diagonal grid pattern along the courtyard building's west wall add an elegant touch to the exposed concrete ends of the structure. Two small one-family houses with gabled roofs sit just west of this building, further emphasizing the pastoral atmosphere.

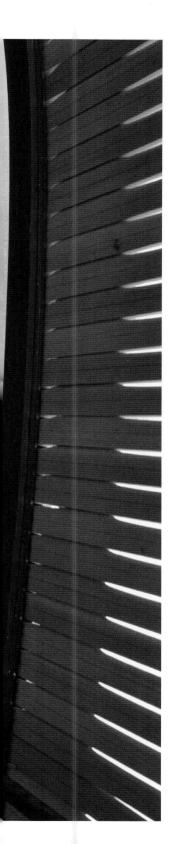

BROCHET
LAJUS PUEYO
RENOVATION
OF THE MUSÉE DE
L'ORANGERIE
2006

Les Nymphéas

Collection
Jean Walter
Paul Guillaume

Bordeaux-based Olivier Brochet pulled off an impressive feat with his renovation of the Musée de l'Orangerie, located in the Tuileries Gardens, west of the Louvre. He helped return the building, a narrow nineteenth-century orangery that became a museum in the 1920s, to its light-filled, historic form, while at the same time making it a very contemporary—and spacious—icon.

The museum, conceived as a home for Monet's *Nymphéas*, has been through several incarnations in its history. The most recent renovation in the 1960s created new second-floor galleries and installed false ceilings, keeping natural light from reaching most of the galleries, including those containing the impressionist flowers (contrary to Monet's original wishes). To reach the paintings, visitors also had to ascend and descend stairs.

Brochet finished his renovation in 2006. He removed the cramped second-floor galleries and built glass walls and a gabled glass and steel roof for most of the building. Sun now pours into the space, similar in size and shape to the original, and visitors can look at the open sky, the Tuileries, and the Seine. In the midst of the scene, Brochet added strikingly contemporary offices inside a white concrete box that seems to hover over the entrance lobby.

Facing the box, a white concrete wall fronts the *Nymphéas*, creating a visual buffer and announcing their importance. A narrow bridge extending from the entrance over a stairway to the basement floors also directs visitors toward the gallery. Above the paintings, the architect installed conical light wells that fill the space with natural light but maintain appropriate levels. Cloth awnings beneath the wells further soften the light. When light levels change, the colors of the *Nymphéas* shift dramatically, producing an incredible effect.

Brochet also added 70,000 square feet of new exhibition space by excavating under the Tuileries to the north as well as new spaces for a shop, theater, and support rooms to the west. The southern half of the long new underground galleries is lit with a long skylight. Exposed concrete walls conflict slightly with the spirit of the art but effectively defer to them. Other, more intimate galleries are painted off-white, maroon, and dark green.

PHILIPPE GAZEAU
EXPANSION OF
LÉON BIANCOTTO
SPORTS COMPLEX
2000

The shell contains first-floor hallways and a large second-floor catwalk that link the complex's spaces. It also contains a new welcome center and a large climbing wall. The grooved polycarbonate surface combines the neighborhood's industrial look with a graceful sleekness that is especially palpable at night. The building glows softly like a lantern and abstract white blurs appear on its exterior as cars on the nearby highway speed by. The grooved surface also creates a visual rhythm, as do the corrugated metal surfaces, the undulating underside of the catwalk, the pitched roof dividers, and the zigzagging skylights above the gym.

The most technically remarkable part of the intervention was the disassembly of the center building's facade, which had been set forward. The firm preserved its wide concrete columns and beams, creating an arresting centerpiece that establishes a link to the project's past.

Within the existing buildings, the architect installed exposed mechanical and ventilation systems and built double-glazed pitched sky-lights above the gym. Exteriors were covered with corrugated metal or painted gray (to match the color of the polycarbonate), and interiors were painted blue. The only additions to the buildings are two white, exposed concrete boxes on both ends of the building that house changing rooms, a welcome desk, and equipment storage spaces.

Located in the northwest corner of Paris, on the edge of the Périphérique—the highway on the site of the city's last walls—Philippe Gazeau's Biancotto Sports Complex unites three unremarkable structures to form one remarkable one. The original complex included a gymnasium, a pool, and a small dance and athletics space, all constructed in the 1940s and separated by parking lots. Gazeau was asked to renovate the buildings, but he took the brief a major step further by connecting the three with an elegant polycarbonate and steel exoskeleton that forms generous intermediary spaces, enlarging the complex and making it more cohesive.

AMELLER & DUBOIS ET ASSOCIÉS
INSTITUTE SUPÉRIEUR DE PARFUM, VERSAILLES
2002

While the idea of studying perfume science may be foreign to many, in France it is serious business. And it's growing. Paris firm Ameller & Dubois was recently commissioned to expand the Institute Supérieur de Parfum, de la Cosmétique, et de l'Aromatique Alimentaire (ISIPCA), founded in 1970 to train future perfume makers and sellers. The campus, in the suburban town of Versailles, had included two beautiful nineteenth-century terra cotta and stucco buildings and a less attractive cement and calcium laboratory building from the 1950s.

The L-shaped addition, composed of two new wings projecting from the existing lab, as well as a new central entrance hall, is built in a horizontal, modernist style. This is an attempt, says Jacques Dubois, to subordinate to the historic buildings, which now function as administrative offices, and to the existing park, a pristine green space with meandering footpaths and large cedar trees. Such sensitivity allowed the school to satisfy the very strict oversight in this wealthy, traditional town, which is, of course, dominated by its famous château.

In cladding the two new wings the firm employed similar materials—terra cotta and concrete—to those employed on the school's existing structures. The wing that houses the library, auditorium, conference rooms, and cafeteria is clad outside and in with elegant reddish horizontal bands of terra cotta. The bands are spaced in front of windows to form brise-soleils. The terra cotta portion feels light, appearing to float above the glass-clad cafeteria, whose transparency helps accentuate the park, in some cases providing clear views through to the surrounding neighborhood.

The classroom and office wing is clad throughout with white concrete, which projects from the windows to form another solar shade and to accentuate the spacing. This section is elevated on concrete columns above administrative offices, and while not transparent, it still maintains a sense of lightness. The rear facade is clad in smooth blue-tinted stone, and its windows are irregularly placed.

An entry area between the wings acts as a mediator and as an extension of each. Thus, the space contains terra cotta, concrete, and calcified stone surfaces, as well as a blackstone floor. A large narrow skylight allows daylight to dominate the space. The space also contains the world's only "Osmothèque," a museum for perfume. The pleasant, although not very ambitious, one-room space, fitted with tropical-wood vitrines designed by the firm, contains about 1,700 scents dating back as far as the first century.

LACATON & VASSAL
PALAIS DE TOKYO
2002

The Palais de Tokyo, across the Seine from the Eiffel Tower, was constructed for the 1937 International Exposition in Paris. It originally held the national modern art collection, which was moved to the Centre Pompidou in 1974. As the Palais de Tokyo took on new uses, its spaces were slowly divided up, and eventually most of the building's original qualities, including the entry of natural light, were lost. The attempted creation of a Palais du Cinema in the late 1990s, a project abandoned during construction, demolished most of the inner walls, drop ceilings, decorative elements, and mechanical systems.

Paris-based Lacaton & Vassal won a 1999 competition to redevelop the massive, 215,000-square-foot space into a setting for contemporary art. The architects chose to keep the building as they found it, retaining its concrete exterior walls and what they call the "splendid industrial waste land" left by the demolition crew.

"The architecture was already interesting when we got there," says Anne Lacaton, who was particularly taken by the contrast between this ruined interior and the ornate stone exterior.

But the choice of minimal intervention was also a necessity. The very modest budget allowed only the very basic necessities, such as handicap entrance ramps, new heating and electrical systems, and building stabilization. Electrical systems and exterior brick and concrete walls were left exposed. Additions, such as the new elevators, were clearly marked and separated from existing areas. The resulting Piranesian spaces are perfect for large installations, which often provide architectural flourishes that the simple structure lacks.

When the project was completed in 2002 the interior was not partitioned, and giant skylights allowed light and warmth inside; natural ventilation, aided by automatically tilting windows, ensured that the space would not become too warm. In subsequent years, exhibitions have called for more partitions, and, as of fall 2006, the temporary closing of the skylights and the ventilation windows.

PEI COBB FREED
EDF TOWER
2001

The La Défense business district, located to the west of Paris, has produced a fascinating—although not always attractive—mix of corporate architecture since its founding in the late 1950s. Easily one of the area's best pieces of architecture is Pei Cobb Freed's EDF tower, built for the French energy giant of the same name and finished in 2001.

The forty-story tower occupies a prominent site in the district, jutting into its center and directly abutting the *dalle*, an elevated pedestrian plaza centered on the axis extending eastward from Johann Otto von Spreckelsen's Grande Arche to the courtyard of the Louvre. To maximize this presence, and to acknowledge the arch, the building is slightly angled to face the monument, which is itself angled 7 degrees off the axis.

The tower is elliptical, a strategy developed to avoid the rectilinear monotony of parallel lines seen in most office buildings and to make it, says Harry Cobb, "less hemmed in by neighboring towers." He continues: "An office tower need not be an overbearing self-referential box, but it can instead be an engaging and responsive presence." Patrick le Cogniac, spokesperson for Hines, the developer, adds that the shape provides almost as much usable space as a rectangular building. The off-center placement of the service core allows space for more open-plan offices on upper floors.

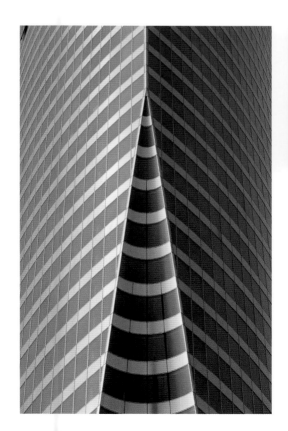

The tower is clad in alternating bands of stainless steel and lightly reflective green glass panels. Both elements reflect changing light conditions. Inside, the glazed lobby—taller and more spacious than those of surrounding buildings—circles the elevator banks. The area is both corporate and elegant, if already somewhat dated. Materials include granite and marble walls and floors, and semiopaque greenish glass over horizontal lines of embossed stainless steel.

Perhaps the most interesting element of the tower is the twenty-six-story concave, cone-shaped opening carved into the building's base. The shape, called the *faille*, or fracture, thrusts inward like the prow of a ship and renders the base invisible from some angles. The *faille* also accommodates a small public gathering place, where people can take in the view from a raised platform beneath a circular awning. "We didn't want the building to stand aloof," says Cobb, who says he felt an obligation to engage the site whenever possible. The steel-framed canopy, 65 feet in diameter, is clad in stainless steel and supported from the building's concrete skeleton, not by columns, and thus appears to hover.

**DIETMAR
FEICHTINGER**
PASSERELLE SIMONE
DE BEAUVOIR
2006

Many considered Dominique Perrault's Bibliothèque Mitterand in the southeast of Paris unsuccessful because it lacked a connection to the rest of the city. Dietmar Feichtinger's Passerrelle de Simone de Beauvoir is an elegant solution to this problem. The multilevel bridge connects the library's raised main court, and the street below, to the beautiful new Parc Bercy, and to the northern quai of the Seine. Both areas are part of emerging neighborhoods in what is one of the most important development zones in the city.

The 1,000-foot-long steel bridge, lined with oak planks, appears almost weightless, spanning the Seine without any intermediate piles. Its fascinating figure-eight shape is produced by the intersection of its main structures, a tensioned steel arch and a convex steel suspension system. The forms are tied together by treelike pilotis called obelisks, laid out every 20 feet, and by long steel beams. Connecting bridges help the form extend to the riverbanks. The structure, says Feichtinger, stresses simplicity over all else. Form and structure are inseparable, and all structural elements are visible. For instance, pieces are welded together, not screwed, emphasizing a continuous form over connected parts.

The bridge curves dramatically from its approach on both banks of the river, which provides varied views toward other parts of the city, including Notre Dame to the west, framed by facing bridges. It also creates small spaces under the arches that will eventually be used for music performances and other events.

The structure holds a magnet-like attraction for passersby, and it is part of the wealth of new activity in the area. A new floating pool just opened next door; Paris Plage, the city's beach rebuilt annually on the banks of the Seine, has been extended to reach near the bridge; and the Batobus, one of the popular tourist cruises, is building a dock for its boats there.

CARBONDALE,
PETER MARINO
ASSOCIATES,
GEORGE SEXTON
ASSOCIATES
LOUIS VUITTON
2005

Located on the ultrachic corner of the Champs-Elysées and avenue George V, about a purse's throw from the Arc de Triomphe, the new Louis Vuitton headquarters in Paris has quickly become one of the most-visited buildings in the city. The 200,000-square-foot store—the company's largest—is contained inside a monumental white 1931 art deco building that is set back from the street on its upper stories and topped by a flat-domed cupola on its northeast corner. Like the company's new stores in Japan and the United States, designed by architects such as Jun Aoki and Kumiko Inui, it may look like a temple to outrageous consumerism. But the building is meant to enhance the Louis Vuitton brand—a combination of classic history and contemporary hipness—through inventive architecture.

Unlike the contemporary facades of Louis Vuitton's other new stores, the building's classic exterior remains intact. But the hipness shows through right away: windows at street level display a rainbow of colored neon lights, set in front of metallic abstractions of the now-omnipresent Louis Vuitton logo. The logo, formed by a circle enclosing the brand's lozenge and flower, can also be seen in horizontal brass rows along the facade, just below the long window sills.

The store does not have a grand entry, but is instead composed of a promenade of long terraces set in a spiral pattern. Architects Carbondale and Peter Marino Associates, along with lighting specialist George Sexton, organized the store into sections that each specialize in different products. Many of the rooms are divided into more manageable spaces by elegant rounded or square dividers formed by metallic LV logos and filled with red glass, white porcelain, leather,

and even wood. The logo also covers many windows, letting light filter through in unusual patterns. Artworks animate the walls, including a mesmerizing video installation by artist James Turrell in which the screen color changes over time.

The highlight of the store is the top-floor luggage room, a skylit, 65-foot-high semicircular space with 1,900 slender stainless-steel rods hanging from the ceiling. These rods become longer as they progress toward the walls, and a full-height mirror gives the illusion of completing the circle. Staring up at the rods, which appear to float in midair, gives a sensation of being inside a sculpture or perhaps an ice palace. Visitors can reach the top floor directly via a 60-foot-long escalator at the back of the store. Designed by artist Tim White-Sobieski, the dark walls of the escalator are covered with over 700,000 fiber-optic points that display a kinetic and colorful video art piece. A pitch-black elevator designed by Danish artist Olafur Eliasson leads visitors to the company's cultural component, a museum featuring artworks based on Louis Vuitton bags by Turrell, architect Zaha Hadid, and designer Marc Jacobs, among others.

IBOS & VITART
FIRE STATION,
NANTERRE
2004

Located in a drab area of Nanterre, a suburb just west of the La Défense business district, this 125,000-square-foot fire station is the headquarters for one of the largest brigades in the region. Its animated facade and dynamic grouping of spaces adds energy to a landscape of characterless housing projects and highway interchanges.

The complex is clearly organized around a U-shaped central courtyard that houses workshops and garages. Trucks enter and leave through large black folding doors on either side of the court. On the south side is a large steel grill that offers views to the street beyond, making the space feel less enclosed; the grill appears to be a solid black sheet unless seen from directly in front, providing security and privacy.

The exterior of the fire station is clad on all sides with a repeating, vertically folding facade of reflective stainless-steel panels. The material not only suits the industrial area, it also supports the architects' goal of adding excitement to a neighborhood where blankness and uniformity prevail. Under the paneling, insulation protects the concrete walls.

The dominant materials inside are exposed concrete, polished concrete, and stainless steel—raw, very strong-looking, some might say masculine, materials that are also, of course, fireproof. The first floor contains offices, a welcome center, a kitchen, and main circulation routes consisting of long exposed concrete hallways painted with dramatic red stripes at eye level. Second-floor halls are lined with firefighter apartments. Rooms have direct ladder access to the first floor so firefighters can get to their trucks in seconds; rooms also have access to a large, slightly reflective stainless-steel box that contains bathrooms.

Perched above the complex is a five-story apartment building, mostly for firefighters' families. The M-shaped structure's open plan admits light and air from the courtyard. Residents enter the apartment building through an inconspicuous perforated screen within the facade. The building is clad with copper-toned aluminum panels, and its aluminum windows frame gold, yellow, orange, and red glass, perhaps ominously intended to evoke fire. The building is divided into three blocks linked by glazed bridges, which house living rooms that open onto south-facing terraces. The rooms are finished in white plaster, a more delicate material than the concrete walls for the firefighters below.

TOYO ITO
COGNACQ-JAY
HOSPITAL
2006

Located in the 15th arrondissement, not far from the Eiffel Tower, Japanese architect Toyo Ito's new Cognacq-Jay Hospital is a peaceful jewel. Replacing an early-twentieth-century facility that had become outdated and outgrown, the building's simple order and embrace of light, nature, and warmth makes it feel like anything but a hospital.

The 35,000-square-foot project includes a T-shaped three-story and a U-shaped five-story rectilinear glass building arranged around a large central courtyard. The south and north facades address the street with double-glazed greenish glass (maximizing privacy and minimizing heat gain) of varying shades arranged in a vibrant,

irregular grid. The windows overlooking the courtyard are either clear or imbedded with a dense, pixellated green pattern evocative of grass and plants.

The north building provides cancer, infectious disease, and physical rehabilitation care. The south building contains a hospice center on the lower floors and a center for autistic children on top. This top level includes a large, open balcony with views of the complex and of the surrounding area.

All patient rooms, and most common spaces, are oriented toward the garden, while hospital offices and support facilities face the street. The simple, meandering Japanese garden contains small pebbles, yellow concrete pathways, reeds, streams, ponds, and contemporary fountains topped with a smooth layer of water. The firm kept several existing chestnut trees and also planted new ones. The streams filter underground toward a rippling waterfall, which feeds into a pool that fronts the north building. The waterfall and the small hill that surrounds it are built over the complex's basement, which connects the two main buildings and contains a chapel as well as laundry, a kitchen, and technical facilities.

Rooms themselves, virtually all designed for single occupancy, are spacious and bright. They include warm details like rounded bathroom doorways clad with blond wood paneling; the same material clads extra-wide hallway walls. Intimate common areas are placed on every floor, a welcome replacement for impersonal waiting rooms. Antique furniture from the original building is used in these spaces. Windows at the end of these hallways extend to the ground to afford maximum views onto the courtyard.

SHIGERU BAN
TEMPORARY OFFICE,
CENTRE POMPIDOU
2004

After winning a competition to design the Centre Pompidou's satellite museum in Metz, France, Japanese architect Shigeru Ban asked the museum if he could build a temporary office inside the building for his Paris team to work on the project. To his surprise, the directors agreed, and the result is a fascinating top-floor space that feels like a combination of a boat, an airplane, and a space-aged architectural folly.

The tubular structure, placed on the small top-floor courtyard and held in place with cinder blocks, measures about 110 feet long and 15 feet wide. It was built by Ban's office, along with an international team of architecture students. A tightly curved vault echoes the form of the Plexiglas walkways on the Pompidou's west facade, including the famous escalator paths that snake up and along its length. The office is covered with a waterproof white membrane on top of plywood sheeting that is supported on a system of cardboard tubes and thin steel bracing on wood joints. The membrane is divided into three waterproof fabric surfaces: PVC (polyvinyl chloride), ETFE (ethylene-tetrafluoroethylene copolymer), and PTFE (polytetrafluoroethylene). The firm used three surfaces in order to test which material would hold up best as the roof of the new Metz building. After two years, the PTFE surface, which covers the north section, showed the least wear, and it will likely cover much of that museum. The surface is perforated at eye level by small, circular Plexiglas windows that look like portholes on a boat. Some swivel for ventilation. The round windows progress in a gridlike fashion up the walls, covering much of the structure. But only the first row is clear; all others are filled in with Styrofoam. The office's white membrane blocks them from sight during the day, but at night the holes glow spectacularly.

Small partitions divide the space from north to south into a reception space, a group work/ conference area, a main office area, and a model-building area. This last area contains large, square windows, the result of a promise by Ban that museum visitors would be able to look into his office at work. While the office was originally planned to be temporary, Ban associate Sachiko Omi reports that the Pompidou may keep it as an exhibition space.

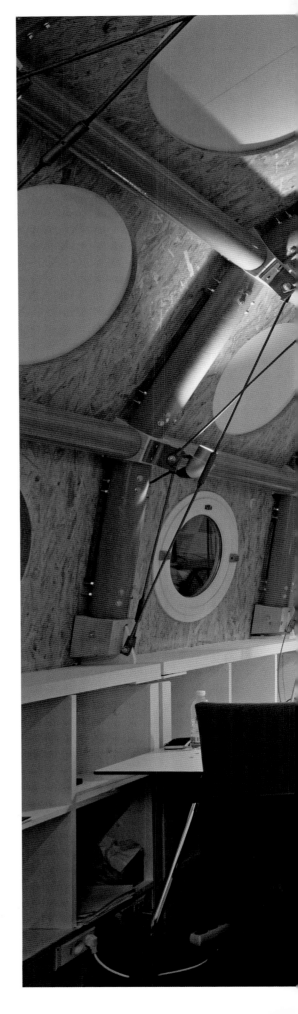

EDOUARD FRANÇOIS
HÔTEL FOUQUET'S
BARRIÈRE
2006

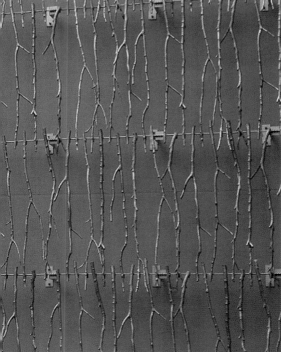

Paris architect Edouard François is never short of innovative ideas. In 2004 he completed the so-called Flower Tower, a concrete apartment building in the northwest of the city that is covered with tall plants, giving the impression that the structure itself is growing. His latest building, the 170,000-square-foot Hôtel Fouquet's Barrière, is even more ambitious.

Located adjacent to avenue George V near the Champs-Elysées, the hotel was built inside an ensemble of interconnected buildings, which were gutted. These include two nineteenth-century structures and a 1980s replica of a Henri IV–style building. An ugly glass-and-steel-covered 1970s structure on the site was torn down. For its replacement François decided to play with the tension between reality and illusion, a common discussion topic in Paris, where new buildings are made to look old while old buildings receive modern interiors. To do this, he made concrete molds of one of the nineteenth-century buildings, copying it piece by piece. After affixing these thin molded forms to a concrete core, the entire surface was painted a uniform dark gray in order to modernize the look of the building and to clarify its falseness. New windows were randomly placed across the facade, thick rectangles with mirrored surrounds, producing a mesmerizing effect for guests looking out.

To maximize the unremarkable courtyard and again manipulate the notion of reality versus fantasy, François commissioned silvery aluminum reproductions of eight thousand wood sticks, which are fashioned into an intricate wall.

Interior decoration was handled by the well-known French interior designer Jacques Garcia, whose contemporary style mixed with classical motifs seems at odds with François's radical thinking. Traditional couches covered with modern fabrics are juxtaposed with minimalist coffee tables. Beige, maroon, and mahogany are mixed with floral patterns. Nonetheless, the ensemble works, perhaps an unintentional, ironic nod to François's challenges of classical re-creation.

PIERRE LOMBARD
PORTE D'ASNIÈRES
PUBLIC HOUSING
2004

Shortly after 2000, architect Pierre Lombard won a competition to build two public housing towers in the northeast corner of a new zone in the northwest of Paris called Porte d'Asnières. The master plan for the area, which is built around a simple new park, was prepared by Christian de Portzamparc, who required that all the building facades present variation and rhythm.

Lombard took this goal to an extreme by dividing his two buildings into six variously sized sections, creating what he calls a "mini-Manhattan," offsetting shorter clean white blocks with tall zinc-clad fragments. This interesting combination breaks down the masses of the two buildings, which total 50,000 square feet. It also leaves room for new patios and balconies and gives most apartments three or four exposures.

The most striking exterior elements are the zinc facades. The metal was carefully plied to reflect light in various directions. The surface glows in bright light and changes color dramatically according to the weather—bright silver in bright light but almost black on gray days. The windows form a uniform grid along the white concrete facades but are more scattered along the zinc faces, a fortunate result of strict fire-code regulations. The apartments themselves, ranging from studios to three bedrooms, are nondescript but spacious, light filled, and well ventilated.

BECKMANN N'THÉPÉ
LA VILLETTE HOUSE
2003

In 2003 the French shelter magazine *A Vivre* organized the construction of temporary prototype houses in the Parc de la Villette in northeast Paris to demonstrate that sophisticated lodgings could be built at reasonable prices. Ironically, one of the houses, designed by Paris firm Beckmann N'Thépé, still stands only because its owner could not afford to have it removed. But this is a good thing, because the house is one of the more fascinating architectural compositions in the city.

Like Bernard Tschumi's famous red follies, located just across a pedestrian promenade, the two-story wood-frame structure is composed of a series of intersecting cubes, voids, and planes. And with its incessant repetition of basic structural forms, the house is also indicative of Sol LeWitt's mesmerizing wood cube installations, Françoise N'Thépé points out.

The long, narrow home is composed of two L-shaped floors, their plans flipped in opposite directions. The wooden frame's horizontal planks protrude from the north and south sides in small groups, becoming progressively longer. Tall H-shaped vertical planks, connected by steel rods, protrude in a repeating pattern from the east and west ends, advancing either downward, in a stairlike progression, or outward.

N'Thépé says she wanted the house, located in a park that is a peaceful oasis within a gritty neighborhood, to speak to both its urban and bucolic surroundings. The facade is covered with what she calls a very ordered version of graffiti. Metal panels of purple, yellow, orange, and blue appear in random intervals on the north and south facades, while an abstract combination of colored and white panels appears on the east and west facades. The house's surface is also clad with thin horizontal wooden slats and with square and rectangular windows of varying opacity. The house is completely white inside, from the plaster walls to the fiberglass-based fabric ceiling. Very colorful furniture has since been removed. A small, self-sustaining rock and plant garden outside wraps the house in a pastoral, yet far-from-lush atmo-sphere that N'Thépé hopes evokes city life as well.

**MURANO HOTELS
DESIGN GROUP**
KUBE HOTEL
2005

The Kube Hotel, located in a tough section of the 18th arrondissement, near Montmartre, takes its name from the geometric shape that dominates its design. In addition, the retro-futuristic hotel has a unifying theme : the juxtaposition of sleek coolness and sexy *chaleur*.

The courtyard of the revamped nineteenth-century building features a large glass and polished-steel cube at its center. Inside, the double-height bar, which also serves as the entry, has stainless-steel gratings, floor-to-ceiling curtains and a long counter made of tarnished silver. Pink fiber-optic spaghetti-strand lights hang down from the ceiling, while black fur lines everything from the cubic seats and shag-carpet sofas to the supporting columns. The black glass walls are animated by a row of plasma-screen televisions.

The mezzanine is lined with more strands of fiber-optic lights, as well as with twisting plastic bubble chairs. But its highlight is the Ice Kube bar, made from twenty-two tons of giant ice blocks. The blocks are lit from below and above by colored LED lights, which give off only low heat and thus will not melt the ice. Upstairs, hallways are jet black. The hotel's forty-one rooms, by contrast, are bright white, with cubes everywhere; even the sink and the toilet are shaped like squares. More furry elements include teddy bears and the occasional fur bench.

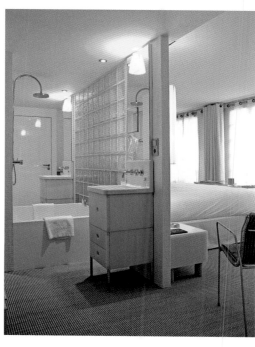